MORE SNIGLETS

RICH HALL & FRIENDS
Illustrated by Arnie Ten

ALPOPUCK *(al' po puk)* n. Any empty dish pushed around the kitchen floor by a dog trying to get the last morsel.

MORE SNIGLETS

(snig' lit):

any word that doesn't appear in the dictionary, but should

Collier Books • Macmillan Publishing Company • New York

"Not Necessarily the News," a production of Not the Network Company, Inc., in association with Moffitt-Lee Productions, is produced by John Moffitt and co-produced by Pat Tourk Lee.

Macmillan Publishing Company
866 Third Avenue, New York, N.Y. 10022
Collier Macmillan Canada, Inc.

Library of Congress Cataloging in Publication Data
Hall, Rich, 1954–
More sniglets.
1. Words, New—English—Anecdotes, facetiae, satire, etc. 2. Vocabulary—Anecdotes, facetiae, satire, etc.
I. Title.
PN6231.W64H33   1985   428.1'0207   84-29200

ISBN 0-02-012560-7
10 9 8 7 6 5 4 3 2 1

Designed by Antler & Baldwin, Inc.
PRINTED IN THE UNITED STATES OF AMERICA

*cover illustration:
MALIBUGALOO (*mal ih boo' guh lew*) n. A dance that affects barefoot beachgoers on hot summer days.

Hand lettering by Bernard Maisner

For Jim and Doris

CONTRIBUTORS

Jason Acquisto Keith Allen Frank Antonowitz Skip Balgemann Stephen Balsamo Richard Banford, Jr. Bobby Joe Barret Matt Besterman Jasper Borgman Greg Bowman Kim R. Brandt Judith Busman Mike Caldwell Dean Carignan Dave Carpenter Brian Clayton Irene Cole Thomas Cole Fred Conklin Elaine Coon Sandra Corigliano Stephen C. Coyle Leigh Cox Frances Curtis Andrea Dalzell Steve Danz Larry Davis David DeRouse Solange DeSantis Bruce Devino Ben Dickinson Steve Dings Margie Dodd Chris Dodson Terry Dugan Debbie Duplantis Brett Ellinsberg Melinda Ellis Pam Entzel Vince Fazzi Brian Fetcie Brian Fitzpatrick Tom Flynn Bill Forrester Tom Foy Bill Francis Bob Frederick Tom Gambaccini Richard Gan Caton Gates Chris Gaydash Ed Gilbert Dennis Gishwiller Steve Gitter Matt Glose Jay Green Kelly Haden **Rich Hall** Phillip Hamilton Michael J. Harris Will Hauptman David Hefferman Susan Helms Kenneth P. Henson Gail Hill Grant Howe Michael Hoyt Scott & Andie Janszen Malcolm & Ann Johnston Russ Josephson Scott Kafora Mike Karlovich Lawrence Kawcak Chris Keefe Ellen Keller Kate Watkins Klein Dan Koenig Bruce Kooken John Kozarich Barbara LaRochelle Dave Lurie Stacy Lynch Mark Majors Bill Mattia Bill May Allison McCarthey Randi McDonald Amanda Rae McNab Beth McShane John Miller Karma Miller Scott Milne Ray & Vikki Moggio Don Moore Nancy Moran Robert Mullins Brett Nagy Maryann Newby Neil Newman Bill Nilsson Mark Barker Nimick Carolyn Null Dan O'Conner Jeff Ogus Chris Ossanna Andy Parent Brent Parker Bruce Parker Mitch Pascal Gina Plude Sharon Potter Mike Rami Carl Reynolds Tony Russo Rick Samuels Michelle Anne Scantling John Schlosser Howard Schoeberlein Daniel Siciliano Tom & Laurie Skiro Emily & Jennifer Slatten Damian & Marian Smeragliualo Tana Sorenson Tom Spatig Louis Spurgeon Michael Stephany Tim Stewart Mike Stuper Roger Taylor Chris Terranova Rich Vanston Mark Vranges Brian Wargen Christa Warner Rona Weisberg E. Annette Wells Steve Wells Rob Whipple Greg Williams Reiko Williamson Rick Wilson Candy Woodyard

CONTENTS

AETS
(ehtz)

n. Greek symbols on water fountain handles.

AGONOSIS
(ag uh no' sis)

n. The syndrome of tuning into "Wide World of Sports" every Saturday just to watch the skier rack himself.

AIRDIRT
(ayr' dirt)

n. A hanging plant that's been ignored for three weeks or more.

ANCHORITY
(an chor' ih tee)

n. A group's final, hard-fought decision on what toppings to order on a pizza.

B+ STAMPEDE
(bee' plus stam peed)

n. The attempt by half the classroom to claim the paper with no name on it.

BACKSPACKLE
(bak' spak uhl)

n. Markings on the back of one's shirt from riding a fenderless bicycle.

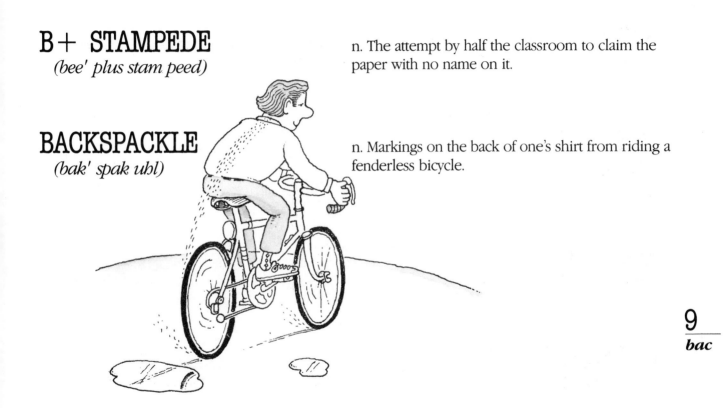

BACKSPUBBLE
(bak' spuh bul)

n. Dishwater that disappears down one drain of a double sink and comes up the other.

BALDAGE
(bald' aj)

n. The accumulation of hair in the drain after showering.

BANECTOMY
(bah nek' to mee)

n. The removal of bruises on a banana.

10
bac

BARGUS
(bar' jus)

n. The area on the windshield that the wipers can't reach.

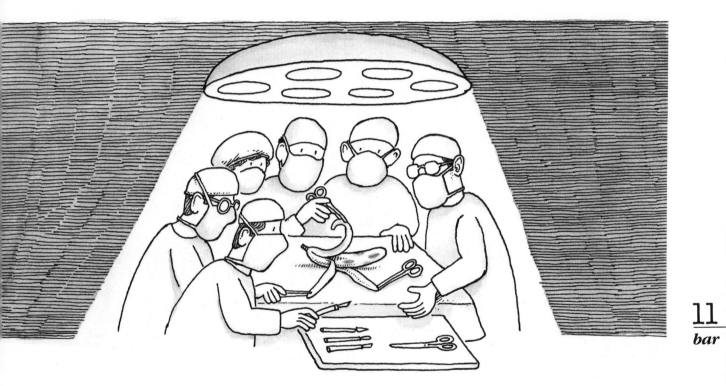

11
bar

BAZOOKACIDAL TENDENCIES

(bah zew' kuh sy dal ten' den seez)

n. The overwhelming desire of most individuals to reach out and pop the gigantic gum bubble billowing from someone's mouth.

BEAVO
(bee' vo)

n. A pencil with teeth marks all over it.

BIMP
(bimp)

n. A blurry or "double-edged" felt-tip marker.

BIXPLEX
(biks' pleks)

n. Psychological block in which a person cannot choose which color of disposable lighter to purchase.

BIZOOS
(bih zews')

n. The millions of tiny individual bumps that make up a basketball.

BLOOAGE
(blew' ij)

n. The residue left on fingers after using an S.O.S. pad.

BLURFLE
(bler' ful)

v. To be caught talking at the top of one's lungs when the music at the bar or disco suddenly stops.

BOMCA
(bahm' ka)

n. A lubricant derived from the salivary gland used for turning book pages.

BOWLIKINETICS
(boh lih kih neh' tiks)

n. The act of trying to control a released bowling ball by twisting one's body in the direction one wants it to go.

BRAZEL
(brah' zul)

n. The scratch plate on a matchbook.

BUBBLIC
(buh' blik)

adj. Addicted to the systematic popping of the bubbles in packing material.

BUGPEDAL
(bug' ped uhl)

v. To accelerate or decelerate rapidly in an attempt to remove a clinging insect from a car's windshield.

BURGACIDE

(burg' uh side)

n. When a hamburger can't take any more torture and hurls itself through the grill into the coals.

BUTTHENGE
(but' henj)

n. A pile of cigarette butts occupying a parking lot space.

BUTTNICK
(but' nik)

n. The crevice on an ashtray where the cigarette rests.

BUZZACKS
(buz' aks)

n. People in phone marts who walk around picking up display phones and listening for dial tones even when they know the phones are not connected.

CAFFIDGET
(ka fij' it)

v. To break up a Styrofoam coffee cup into several hundred pieces after consuming its contents.

17
caf

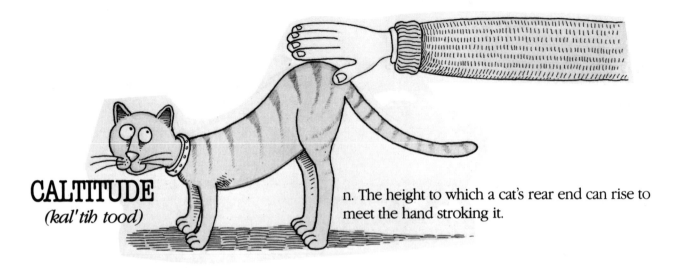

CALTITUDE
(kal' tih tood)

n. The height to which a cat's rear end can rise to meet the hand stroking it.

CARPERIMETER
(kar pur ihm' ih tur)

n. The zone between the wall and the end of the vacuum cleaner where dirt is "safe."

CATLAPSE
(kat' laps)

n. The amount of time a cat sleeping on his owner's lap has to awake and prepare to hit the floor before the owner stands up.

CELLOSTATIC
(sel oh stat' ik)

adj. The electrical property of cracker and cigarette wrappers that causes them to stick to your hand.

CHAIN GANG WALK
(chayn gang wok)

n. Activity observed in the footwear section of cheap department stores where the shoes are wired together "for your convenience."

CHECKUARY
(chek' yew air ee)

n. The thirteenth month of the year. Begins New Year's Day and ends when a person stops absent-mindedly writing the old year on his checks.

CHEERIOMAGNETIZATION
(cheer ee oh mag net i zay' shun)

n. The tendency of the last four or five Cheerios in the bowl to cling together for survival.

CHICLEXODUS
(chik ul eks' oh dus)

n. Any attempt by a gum ball to sneak out of the chute and roll past the buyer.

CHIPFAULT
(chip' fawlt)

n. The stress point on a potato chip where it breaks off and stays behind in the dip.

CHUBBLE
(chub' bul)

n. The aerobic movement combining deep-knee bends and sideward hops used when trying to fit into panty hose.

CIRCUMPOPULATE
(sur kum pop' yew layt)

v. To finish off a popsicle "laterally" because the "frontal" approach causes one to gag.

COMBILOOPS
(kom' bih lewps)

n. The two or three unsuccessful passes before finally opening a combination locker.

CORNICLE
(kor' nih kul)

n. Breaded "washer" left on the stick after eating a corndog.

COUNTERSAURUS
(kown tur sawr' us)

n. Any person who orders two pieces of cheesecake and a Tab.

THE CRANIAL STOMP
(the kray' nee uhl stomp)

n. A somewhat primitive dance performed by youngsters trying to step on the heads of their shadows.

CRAYOLLIA
(kray oh' lee uh)

n. The area on the refrigerator where kindergarten drawings are displayed.

CRINKS
(krinks)

n. Crevices and junctions where car wax gets in but doesn't get out.

CRUMBPLUMB
(krum' plum)

v. To attack a cereal box in an attempt to retrieve the prize.

CUBELO
(kyew' beh lo)

n. The one cube left by the person too lazy to refill the ice tray.

CUSHUP
(kush' up)

v. To sit down on a couch somehow causing the cushion next to you to rise.

DARF
(darf)

n. The least attractive side of a Christmas tree that ends up facing the wall.

DIGITRITUS
(dij ih tree' tus)

n. Deposits found between the links of a watchband.

DILLRELICT
(dil rel' ikt)

n. The last pickle in the jar that avoids all attempts to be captured.

DIMP
(dimp)

n. A person who insults you in a cheap department store by asking "do you work here?"

DIPWAVERS
(dip' way vurz)

n. People who raise their hands when riding on roller coasters.

DOGNUT
(dawg' nut)

n. The giant nut on the side of a fire hydrant.

DOORK
(dawrk)

n. A person who always pushes on a door marked "pull" or vice versa.

DOWNPAUSE
(down' pawz)

n. The split second of dry weather experienced when driving under an overpass during a storm.

DROOT
(drewt)

n. A Dorito with an unnatural fold in it.

DRYLOWGRAPHS
(dry' loh grafs)

n. Strange, unintelligible symbols that accompany the washing instructions on clothing labels.

EASTROTURF
(ee' stroh terf)

n. The artificial grass in Easter baskets.

EIFFELITES
(eye' ful eyetz)

n. Gangly people sitting in front of you at the movies who, no matter what direction you lean in, follow suit.

ELEVERTIGO
(el uh vur' tig oh)

n. The sensation one experiences when an elevator stops or takes off too suddenly.

ELMERDERMIS
(el mur durm' is)

n. The white sheath that surrounds the nozzle of a glue dispenser.

ESCALOS
(es' kah lohz)

n. People who always end up taking the long way around from escalator to escalator when moving from floor to floor in shopping malls.

EUFIRSTICS
(yew fur' stiks)

n. Two people waiting on the phone for the other to hang up first.

EXASPIRIN
(eks as' prin)

n. Any bottle of pain reliever with an impossible-to-remove cotton wad at the top.

EXECUGLIDE

(eks ek' yew glyd)

v. To propel oneself about an office without getting up from the chair.

FERROLES
(fer' olz)

n. The holes in the bottom of a steam iron.

FETCHPLEX
(fech' pleks)

n. State of momentary confusion in a dog whose owner has faked throwing the ball and palmed it behind his back.

FICTATE
(fik' tayt)

v. To inform a television or screen character of impending danger under the assumption they can hear you.

FINNAGE
(fin' aj)

n. The act of watching your money swallowed up as your groceries ride the conveyor belt at the supermarket.

FLARPSWITCH
(flarp' swich)

n. The one light switch in every house with no function whatsoever.

FLIMPS
(flimps)

n. People (usually observed in waiting rooms) who have advanced the Evelyn Wood technique to the point where they can flip through a magazine without ever looking down from the clock.

FLINTSTEP
(flint' step)

v. To wind up one's feet before running away in fear. Common among cartoon characters.

FLURRANT
(fluhr' uhnt)

n. The one leaf that always clings to the end of the rake.

FAMAMAGE
(fa mam' aj)

v. To eliminate any annoying engine noise by simply turning up the volume of the radio.

FODS
(fahdz)

n. Couples at amusement parks who wear identical T-shirts, presumably to keep from getting lost.

FOYS
(foyz)

n. Missing pieces of a jigsaw puzzle that you later find stuck to the underside of your arm.

FRANKFLUID
(frank flew' id)

n. The liquid at the bottom of hot dog packages.

FRUSTRA
(frus' trah)

n. The special plastic used in the manufacture of fast-food ketchup packets.

FUFFLE
(fuh' ful)

v. To assume, when dining out, that you are making things easier on the waitress by using the phrase "when you get a chance . . .".

35
fuf

FURBULA
(fer' byew luh)

n. The designated chewing area on a dog's back.

GANGLOOT
(gan' glewt)

n. Person who leaves all his ski passes on his jacket just to impress people.

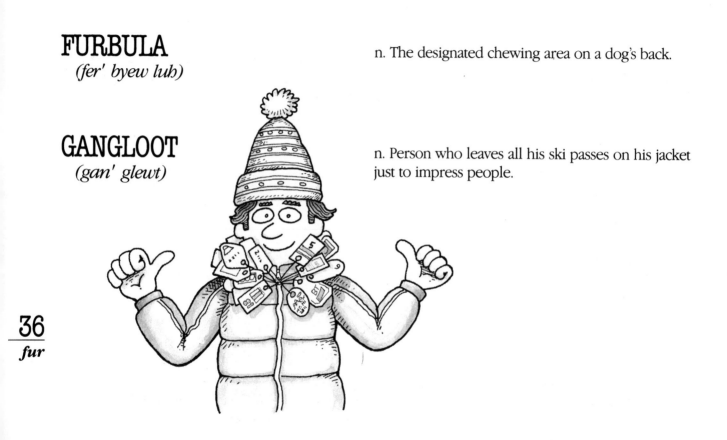

GAPIANA
(ga pee ah' nah)

n. The unclaimed strip of land between the "you are now leaving" and "welcome to" signs when crossing state lines.

GAZINTA (÷)
(gah zin' tuh)

n. Mathematical symbol for division; also the sound uttered when dividing out loud. (Example: "Four *gazinta* eight twice.")

GIBBLE
(jib' buhl)

n. The sliding keyhole cover on a car trunk.

GIZZLEDIPPLERS
(gih' zul dip lurz)

n. Those annoying waving hands seen on the backs of Winnebagos (placed there by people too lazy to be friendly on their own).

GLAMP
(glamp)

n. The telescopic device used to retrieve golf balls from ponds.

GLUTE
(glewt)

v. To shake a sugar packet vigorously so as to move the contents to the bottom before tearing open.

GRANTNAP
(grant' nap)

n. The extra five minutes of sleep you allow yourself that somehow makes all the difference in the world.

GREEDLING
(gree' dling)

v. Pretending to read the inscription on the birthday card when you really just want to know how much the check is for.

GRINTIGER
(grin' tuh jer)

n. The numbered code on the back of a greeting card that, when deciphered, reveals the price.

GUMMERATOR
(gum' uhr ay ter)

n. The pointed rubber object on the end of some toothbrushes.

GYROPED
(jy' roh ped)

n. A kid who cannot resist spinning around on a diner stool.

HACULA
(hak' yew luh)

n. The last few inches of tape measure or lawn mower cord that refuses to rewind automatically.

HALVENT
(hav' ent)

n. A style of auto window, found in later models, that only rolls down halfway.

HOUNDWOUNDING
(hownd' wown ding)

n. Canine act of circling a spot three or four times before settling on it.

HUDNUT
(hud' nuht)

n. The leftover bolt or screw in any "some assembly required" project.

ICISION
(ih sih' zhun)

n. Delicate operation performed on Neapolitan-flavored ice cream in which one entire flavor is precisely and systematically removed. (See **KNUCK**.)

INKSLICK
(ink' slik)

n. A greasy spot on a piece of stationery or test paper.

IRANT
(eye' rant)

n. A seamless pistachio nut; a pistachio nut afraid to come out in public.

JAVA-VU
(jah' vah-voo)

n. Phenomenon of constantly adjusting the sugar/cream level of your coffee to your liking, only to have a waitress come along and ruin it again.

JOES OF ARC
(johz' uhv ark)

n. Tiny drops of Mr. Coffee that die on the burner after the pot is removed.

JUKEJITTERS
(jook' jit erz)

n. Fear that everyone thinks you picked the awful tune emanating from the jukebox when it was actually the person before you.

KAWASHOCK
(kah wah shahk')

n. Pulling into the last remaining parking spot only to discover a motorcycle there.

KEYFRUIT
(kee' froot)

n. The one apple, pear, or tomato in the stand that, when removed, causes all the others to tumble forward.

KNUCK
(nuk)

n. Ice cream collected on the back of the hand when scraping the last portions from the box.

KROGLING
(kroh' gling)

n. The nibbling of small items of fruit and produce at the supermarket, which the customer considers "free sampling" and the owner considers "shoplifting."

LIMALOPE
(ly' muh lohp)

n. The disgusting foreskin on a lima bean.

LINENEE
(lih nen ee')

n. The member of a two-person folding team at the Laundromat who takes the sheet and completes the fold.

LODGECOMBING
(loj' coh ming)

n. Final reconnaissance before vacating a motel room.

LOGGIUM
(log' yum)

n. Water that drips from one's nose hours after swimming.

LOOMLIES
(lewm' leez)

n. Jockey shorts that have lost their elasticity.

LORP
(lawrp)

n. The part of the shoe that collapses when you try to pull it on without a shoehorn.

47
lor

mag

MAGNAGRAM
(mag'nuh gram)

n. Any sign that takes on a new meaning when a magnetic letter falls off.

MALIBUGALOO
(mal ih boo' guh lew)

n. A dance that affects barefoot beachgoers on hot summer days.

MALTIAN
(mal' shun)

n. The alien beside you with concave cheeks, bulging forehead veins, and clearly outlined skull who is sucking on a too thick milk shake.

MANILLIUM
(mah nil' ee yum)

n. The lifespan of the clasp on a manila envelope before it breaks off and dies.

MICROTREK
(my' kro trek)

n. Any nervous trip to the microwave oven to make sure the food hasn't incinerated.

MICROTS
(my' krotz)

n. The two thumbnail-sized pieces you end up with when trying to remove a paper towel in a public washroom.

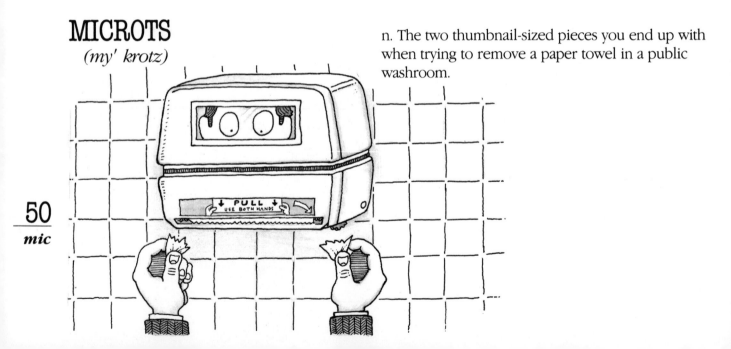

MIMOIDS
(mim' oydz)

n. People addicted to the smell of newly mimeographed test papers.

MISCORDANCE
(mis kawr' dans)

n. The principle that states: when reaching for drape cords, you will always tug on the wrong one first, practically tearing down the whole contraption.

MOPEEPS
(moh' peeps)

n. People compelled to look through the curtain opening of your motel room as they pass by.

MOTMESHS
(maht' mesh ez)

n. A pair of inseparable shopping carts.

MOTODRIFT
(moh' toh drift)

n. The mistaken belief at a stoplight that your car is moving backward when, actually, the car beside you is moving forward.

MOZZALASTICS
(maht suh las' tiks)

n. Large deposits of cheese that stick to the top of the pizza box.

MULTIPOCHOHOLES
(mul ti po' cho holz)

n. Wounds left in test papers from overerasing.

MUMMABOLIC CHORUS
(mum uh bah' lik ko' rus)

n. When three or more people are singing along to a tune and suddenly discover they are all faking their way through the unintelligible lyrics.

MUMMELOT
(muh' muh laht)

n. The bottomless repository where theatre tickets are dropped.

NEGATILE
(neh' guh tyl)

n. An area of the bathroom floor where, somehow, the scale registers you five pounds lighter.

NEOICE
(nee oh ice')

n. Any ice cube removed before its time that, upon close examination, resembles a carpenter's level.

NEUTRON PEAS
(new' tron peez)

n. Tiny green objects in TV dinners that remain frozen even when the rest of the food has been microwaved beyond recognition.

NEWTON
(new' tin)

n. The cookie shell surrounding the fig in a Fig Newton.

NICOMETEOR

(nik oh mee' tee awr)

n. A cigarette that exits through a car's front window and reenters through the back.

NIFLECK
(nib' flek)

n. The unmarked domino in the set.

NIZZLEBRILL
(nib' zuhl bril)

n. The "night-day" switch on a rearview mirror.

NOCTURNUGGETS
(nok' ter nuh gitz)

n. Deposits found in one's eye upon awakening in the morning, also called: GOZZAGAREENA, OPTIGOOK, EYEHOCKEY, etc.

NOFLET
(nahf' lit)

n. The upward swirl of hair found on certain individuals such as Ronald Reagan and Big Boy.

NURGE
(nerj)

v. To inch closer to a stoplight thinking that will cause it to change quicker.

110 AT THE EQUATOR
(won' ten at the ek way' tawr)

n. Any burning sensation experienced directly below the navel when putting on a pair of jeans straight from the dryer.

OOPZAMA
(ewp' za muh)

n. Sudden scratching of scalp or face upon realization that the person you were waving at isn't who you thought it was.

OPUP
(op' uhp)

v. To push one's glasses back on the nose.

OREOSIS
(awr ee oh' sis)

n. The practice of eating the cream center of an Oreo before eating the cookie outsides.

OTISOSIS
(oh tis oh' sis)

n. The inability to meet anyone else's eyes in an elevator.

PAJANGLE
(pah jan' gul)

n. Condition of waking up with your pajamas turned 180 degrees.

P.A.T. (PERCUSSIVE ACCORDION-TROMBONE) METHOD
(pee ay tee   meth' uhd)

n. Standard approach to preparing a straw for use. Consists of driving it sharply downward against a table top, thus causing the wrapper to rip open and achieve an "accordion" effect. The user then brings the exposed end of the straw to his mouth and blows the wrapper across the room.

PEDAERATION
(ped air ay' shun)

n. Perfect body heat achieved by having one leg under the sheet and one hanging off the edge of the bed.

PEPPIÉR
(pehp ee ay')

n. The waiter at a fancy restaurant whose sole purpose seems to be walking around asking diners if they want ground pepper.

PERCAMBULATE
(pur kam' byew layt)

v. Tendency of fitted sheets to lose their grip and roll up the mattress.

PERMAPRESSION
(pur' muh preh shun)

n. The discovery that there is no real difference in the various cycles of your washing machine.

PETONIC
(peh ton' ik)

adj. One who is embarrassed to undress in front of a household pet.

PHILOPOLOGIST
(fil ah pahl' ah jist)

n. A specialist who loads people onto amusement rides.

PIELIBRIUM
(py lih' bree uhm)

n. The point at which the crust on a wedge of pie outweighs the filling and tips it over.

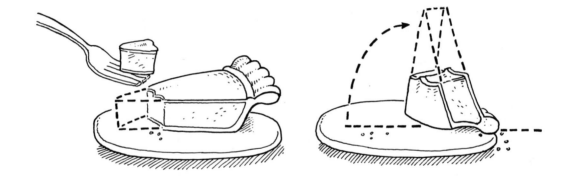

PIEPUSHERS
(py' puh shurz)

n. Attendants at fast food restaurants who, no matter what you order, try to unload apple or cherry turnovers on you.

PIEWAGON
(py' wa gun)

n. The small vehicle that carries game pieces around a Trivial Pursuit board.

PIGSLICE
(pig' slys)

n. The last unclaimed piece of pizza that everyone is secretly dying for.

POCKALANCHE
(pok' uh lansh)

n. Perpetual action of reaching down to pick up an item fallen from a shirt pocket, only to have another item fall out.

POLARIND
(poh' luh rynd)

n. The peeling on a Polaroid snapshot.

PORCELATOR
(pawr' suh lay tawr)

n. The hole near the rim of a bathroom sink.

POSICRO
(pah' sih kro)

n. The magnetic or "charged" strip of Velcro. *ant* NEUCRO (new' kro) n. The negative or "uncharged" strip of Velcro that *Posicro* adheres to.

POSTALPORTS
(poh' stuhl pawrtz)

n. The annoying windows in envelopes that never line up with the address.

PREMADERCI
(pree muh dayr' chi)

n. The act of saying goodbye to someone, then running into him again moments later (usually accompanied by a lame quip such as "you following me?").

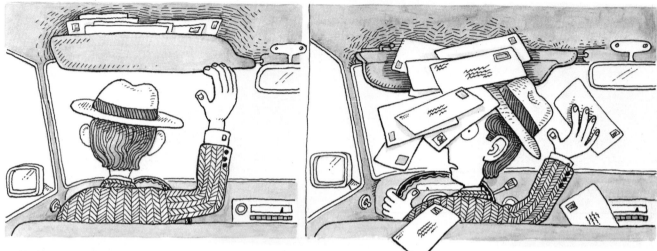

PREMAIL
(pree' mayl)

n. Mail that is placed behind the visor in the car and left for several months before it is finally sent.

PRETZALINE
(pret sah leen')

n. The salt deposit at the bottom of a bag of pretzels.

PRIMPO
(prim' po)

n. A person who passes a mirror then has to step back, presumably to reassure himself he still exists.

P-SPOT
(pee' spaht)

n. The area directly above the urinal in public restrooms that men stare at, knowing a glance in any other direction would arouse suspicion.

PULPID
(puhl' pid)

n. A kid who enjoys the carton more than the item that came in it.

PULPULARITY
(puhl pyew lahr' ih tee)

n. Molecular property of newspaper clippings that allows them to tear evenly north to south but jaggedly east to west.

PUNTIFICATE
(puhn tih' fih kayt)

v. To try to predict in what direction a football will bounce.

PUPSQUEAK
(puhp' skweek)

n. The sound a yawning dog emits when it opens its mouth too wide.

RAMPRIOT
(ramp' ry uht)

n. Free-for-all that erupts as soon as the stewardess utters the phrase "please remain in your seats until the plane has come to a complete stop."

71
ram

RELED
(ree led')

v. To reset all the digital clocks in the household following a power failure.

ROEBINKS
(roh' binks)

n. Those mysterious chimes you always hear in department stores.

ROHRSHIRT
(roar' shurt)

n. A shirt with an ink stain on the pocket.

RUBBAGE
(ruh' bij)

n. Large pieces of truck tire found on the side of the road.

SCHWIGGLE
(shwi' gul)

n. The amusing rotation of one's bottom while sharpening a pencil.

SCRIBBLICS
(skrib' bliks)

n. Warm-up exercises designed to get the ink in a pen flowing.

SERVELENCE
(surv' lents)

n. The sudden lull in conversation that occurs at a table of diners when the food is served.

SHOCKLET
(shahk' lit)

n. The seldom-used third hole on an electrical outlet.

SHUZMA
(shuhz' muh)

n. The portion of window cleaner that the spray tube can no longer reach.

SLOPWEAVER
(slahp' wee vuhr)

n. Someone who has mastered the art of repositioning the food on his plate to give the appearance of having consumed a good portion of it.

SLOTTERY AND VENDICATION
(slot' er ee and ven' di kay shun)

n. A public misdemeanor in which a person gambles on a vending machine, loses, and tries to exact revenge by kicking it.

SLURCH
(slerch)

n. The combination "ouch" and slurping noise one makes when eyeing someone else's bad sunburn.

SNACKMOSPHERE
(snak' moh sfeer)

n. The empty but explosive layer of air at the top of a potato chip bag.

SNARGLE
(snar' gul)

v. To lessen the visual impact of a horror movie by filtering it through one's fingers.

SNUGGAGE
(snuh' gaj)

n. The act of retying both shoestrings when only one needed it.

SOMNAMBAPOLOGIST
(som nam ba pol' uh jist)

n. Person too polite to admit he was sleeping even when awakened at three in the morning.

SPAGELLUM
(spa gel' um)

n. The loose strand on each forkful of spaghetti that beats one about the chin and whiskers.

SPOOD
(spewd)

n. Flat wooden "spoon" that accompanies ice cream cups.

SPROUT LINES
(sprowt lynz)

n. Visible lines at the bottom of trouser legs where the hems have been let down.

SPUDRUBBLE
(spud' ruhb uhl)

n. Unclaimed french fries at the bottom of a fast food bag.

SQUAFFELS
(skwa' felz)

n. The individual squares comprising a waffle.

SQUANDERPRINT
(skwan' duhr print)

n. Directions that try to make you use up a product faster than you normally would. (Ex.: Apply shampoo. Lather. Rinse. Repeat.)

SQUATFLECTION
(skwat' flek shun)

n. The distorted reflection in a car window that makes you resemble a midget wrestler.

SQUATIC DIVERSION
(skwa' tik dy vur' zhun)

n. Any pretended activity that commands a dog owner's attention while the dog relieves itself on a neighbor's lawn.

SQUIGGER
(skwig' uhr)

n. A cherry tomato that explodes upon contact with a fork.

SUBATOMIC TOASTICLES
(sub ah tom' ik toh' stik uhlz)

n. Tiny fragments of toast left behind in the butter.

TABLE SNORKELING
(tay' bul snawrk' ling)

n. Frantic gesticulations when one bites into hot food and has to take in air to cool it off.

TELLETIQUETTE
(tel et' ih ket)

n. The polite distance kept by one person behind another at an automatic teller machine (so as not to be suspected of trying to glimpse that person's secret code).

TELOUSTIC
(tel oo' stik)

adj. The tendency for people to shout into the phone when calling long distance.

TESTLICE
(test' lys)

n. Those tiny bugs that invade your hair when you're taking an exam.

TOILET TOUPEE
(toy' lit too pay')

n. Any shag carpet toilet cover that causes the lid to become top-heavy, thus creating endless annoyance to male users.

TOOLCENTRIC
(tewl sen' trik)

adj. Describes any tool that, when dropped, rolls to the exact center of the car's underside.

TRIDECKPICK
(try dek' pik)

n. A miniature sword or similar device used to hold a sandwich together.

TUBSWIZZLE
(tub' swih zuhl)

v. To slide oneself back and forth in the bathtub in order to mix the too hot water with the cooler water.

TURFIGEE AND PEDIGEE
(ter' fih jee and ped' ih jee)

n. The two extreme target points of a rotary lawn sprinkler, TURFIGEE being the safest point at which to walk past, PEDIGEE being the most dangerous.

TWINKIDUE
(twin' kee dew)

n. The residue on the inside of the wrapper that every junk food addict eventually gets to.

UCLIPSE
(yew' klips)

n. The dangerous arc into another lane made by drivers just before executing a turn.

UMBILINKUS
(uhm bih link' us)

n. The tiny appendage at the end of a link sausage.

UMBRACE
(uhm' brays)

n. The small strap that holds an umbrella in place.

UNDERHOODIST
(un dur hood' ist)

n. A service station attendant with a genius for locating hood latches.

UNFARE
(un fayr')

n. The dollar you owe the cab driver before you've even moved a foot.

UNIPEA
(yew' ni pee)

n. A peanut with only one compartment.

VACATION ELBOW
(vay kay' shun el' bo)

n. A condition that suddenly develops in a father's arm during a vacation trip that allows him to reach out and slap you from incredible distances.

VEGELUDES
(vej' eh loodz)

n. Individual peas or kernels of corn that you end up chasing all over the plate.

VENDOMETRIC
(ven doh meh' trik)

n. A person who inserts his change in a vending machine according to size (dimes, nickels, quarters).

VENDOVALUEIST
(ven doh val' yew ist)

n. A person who inserts his change according to value (nickels, dimes, quarters).

VOITLOCK
(voyt' lok)

n. When the basketball gets lodged between the rim and the backboard.

WAFTIC
(wahf' tik)

adj. Describes any person in whose direction campfire or barbeque smoke always blows.

WERDLE
(wurd' uhl)

v. To lean over the edge of a train or subway platform in search of the oncoming vehicle. WERDLEMASS (n.)—an entire group of people leaning over a train or subway platform.

WISKAGE
(wis' kaj)

n. The gravitational property that causes clothes to stick to the outside of the drum after the spin cycle.

WOOWAD
(wew' wad)

n. Giant clumps of stuck-together rice served at Chinese restaurants.

XEROXPOX
(zee' roks poks)

n. Skin disease of copier paper, characterized by the appearance of large black powdery blotches.

YOTATE
(yoh' tayt)

v. To allow a yo-yo to unwind itself.

ZEBRALANE
(zee' bruh layn)

n. The striped area between the interstate and the turnoff lane where cars go when drivers can't decide what to do next.

ZEEPT
(zeept)

n. The accumulation of dead insects around an electric bug fryer.

ZERBLOT
(zur' blaht)

n. The last kid picked in any neighborhood sporting event.

ZIPCUFFED
(zip' cuft)

v. To be trapped in one's trousers by a faulty zipper.

How to Use Your Sniglets Videodisc

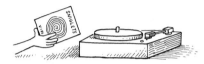

1. Remove disc along dotted line and place on any turntable.

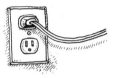

2. Make sure turntable is plugged into electrical outlet.

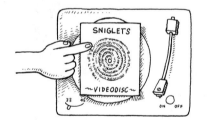

3. Using finger, rotate platter of turntable in a counterclockwise direction. View sniglets.

4. When you have completed viewing the sniglets, you may rewind the disc by rotating it in the opposite direction.

Videodisc

Sniglets

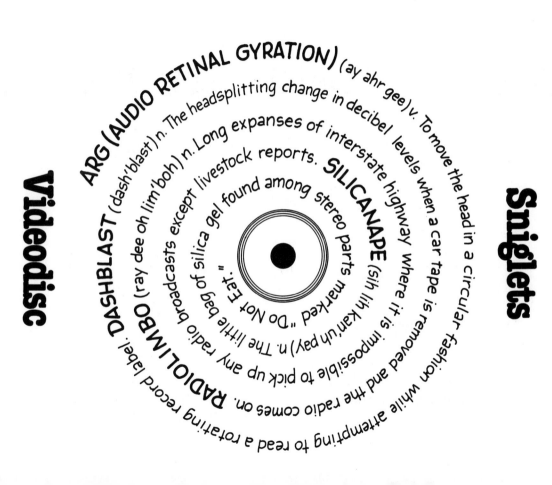

ARG (AUDIO RETINAL GYRATION) (ay ahr gee) v. To move the head in a circular fashion while attempting to read a rotating record label.

DASHBLAST (dash'blast) n. The headsplitting change in decibel levels when a car tape is removed and the radio comes on.

RADIOLIMBO (ray dee oh lim'boh) n. Long expanses of interstate highway where it is impossible to pick up any radio broadcasts except livestock reports.

SILICANAPE (sih lih kan'uh pay) n. The little bag of silica gel found among stereo parts marked "Do Not Eat."

OFFICIAL SNIGLETS ENTRY BLANK

Dear Rich:

    Here's my contribution to the English language. I'm sure it's as good as yours:

_____

_____

_____

_____

_____

Sincerely,

(name)   _____

(street address)   _____

(city, state, zip code) _____

SNIGLETS
P.O. Box 2350
Hollywood, CA 90078

Idiot
Box